The Secret To Profitable Business Ideas

DEXX WILLIAMS

This report is designed to provide information in regard to the subject matter covered. It is sold with the understanding that the publisher, author, and advisers are not rendering legal, accounting or other professional services.

Every effort has been made to make this report as complete and as accurate as possible. However, there may be mistakes, both typographical and in content. Therefore, this text should be used only as a general guide and not as the ultimate source of published information. Furthermore, this report contains information only up to the printing date.

The authors, advisers and publisher shall have neither liability nor responsibility to any person or entity with respect to any loss or damage caused, or alleged to be caused, directly or indirectly, by the information contained in this manual.

With that out of the way, let's continue with the exciting marketing strategies that successful businesses are using to increase their profits!

To My Friends,

My drive to help others around the world to achieve their dreams and be successful is enhanced due to the incredible family and friends I have been blessed to have in my life. While there are far too many of you to list, please realize I appreciate all of you much more than you know. Here are just a few I must acknowledge for their continuous support:

Leanorah, Ava, Jaida, Jim and Liz, my sources of inspirations in life, thank you for your love and for always being there when I need you. Words can't express how much you mean to me.

Stan D., thank you for always pushing me to think even bigger about what is possible and for constantly challenging me to do better even when you don't realize you're doing so.

Last, but definitely not least, Ryan L., a loyal friend, mentor, and constant source of knowledge and thought-provoking ideas. You've changed how I approach problem solving in more ways than even I probably realize. Thank you for your unwavering confidence in my abilities and influential leadership.

CONTENTS

My Dramatic Breakthrough

If you want to ensure that your new business idea will be extremely profitable…

If you're looking to add a profitable new revenue source to an existing business…

Or if you just want the ability to identify profitable investment opportunities from those that are doomed to fail from the start…

Then you will soon realize this is…

THE BOOK YOU HAVE BEEN WAITING FOR

By taking advantage of the information contained within the following pages, you will have more control and influence within any industry you choose.

You will be able to leverage the strategies I'll be sharing with you to not only enhance your social status and strengthen your relationships with potential industry partners, but also to obtain recognition and acknowledgement from within your industry for developing innovative new ideas, all of which I'll be showing you how to do.

But first, you may be wondering who I am and why I decided to create this book.

My name is Dexx Williams, I live in Alberta, Canada, and I help businesses to increase their sales by 30% or more in as little as 30 days – even if they've been struggling to generate improved sales for years.

I created this book because the sad reality is statistically…

BUSINESSES TYPICALLY DIE
WITHIN THEIR FIRST 18 MONTHS

Unless their owners take proper steps to prevent this from happening (*like you are by reading this book)*!

Why do I say that? It's simple, really. Most business owners essentially come up with the idea to start a business, get the money together for inventory and supplies, and then open their doors. If they're lucky, they will have picked a convenient location or pricing model in the market that allows them to generate some decent money for a couple of years.

However, most of the time those businesses only survive because their customers find them convenient to purchase from, maybe just due to their prices or location and not because they offer anything significantly better than their competitors.

What usually happens next? A competing business opens their doors in the same market, but implements the strategies I outline within this book. Soon this new competitor begins dominating the market easily, taking massive portions of market share and sales away from the "convenient companies" that were surviving previously.

What is the end result? Well, as I stated, according to a 2013 study conducted by Bloomberg.com, 8 out of 10 entrepreneurs who start a business fail within the first 18 months.

HAVING A GOOD BUSINESS IDEA IS NOT ENOUGH

Do you happen to have a proven plan in place to prevent the same fate for your business? If you think that just because you're motivated, have a "good idea," and able to gather up the money to get started, that you'll succeed in business with hard work and positive thinking, you're in for a shock. There's an 80% chance you will fail and lose all the time and money you put into your business – a devastating reality that many business owners have learned the hard way.

This is probably the reason so many aspiring business owners are too scared to even dip their big toe in the "entrepreneurial pool": the fear of losing precious time, money, and more importantly, respect in the eyes of those they care about.

But what if there was a marketing weapon that would give any business the upper hand, something that those failed businesses lacked but that their successful competitors were able to access and crushed them with? Would that be something you'd be interested in having?

Yes? Good. This is exactly why I created this book for you.

After watching many of my friends and family members struggle with their dreams to start and succeed with businesses of their own, some of them nearly losing their homes to devastating debt and eventual bankruptcy, I decided to do some research. I was determined to discover the answer to the question…

WHAT SEPARATES SUCCESSFUL BUSINESSES FROM THOSE THAT FAIL HORRIBLY?

Since 2007, I've been studying strategies used by over 10,000 businesses in over 400 different industries. These strategies have consistently generated profitable results for the businesses that have implemented them in a variety of ways.

The concepts I discovered aren't based on the latest trends, or on available technology, at the time. No. Instead they are based on human nature and sales psychology. In fact, these same strategies have generated results for decades, regardless of industrial or economic factors.

It quickly became clear to me that the secret to profitable success in business wasn't a matter of luck or creativity, but actually just a matter of applying a series of proven business marketing concepts the correct way.

Now I'm on a mission to help as many businesses avoid the fatal business traps that prevent 80% of them from ever becoming successful, and at the same time, share proven business and marketing strategies to generate over $1 billion in new sales for the businesses that utilize my Unique Profit Systems to grow and dominate in their markets.

What does this mean for you? It means I've spent years to create this simple but powerful resource to help show you…

HOW TO POUR MONEY BACK
INTO YOUR BANK ACCOUNT

Basically, it means that this book will be the ultimate shortcut for you, not only in terms of time saved discovering these same powerful strategies, but also on how to apply them for maximum results.

With the help of this book, you will be able to generate profitable business ideas for any market, even if you have no previous experience or knowledge in that market. As you can imagine, the potential is powerful in the right hands.

Whether you are looking to start a new business to obtain financial independence, improve an existing business by adding additional sources of revenue, or identify profitable investment opportunities in a business idea being pitched to you...

THIS BOOK WILL BE YOUR
SECRET MARKETING WEAPON

A profitable tool that will help you accumulate market share quickly, while placing the competitors in your market at a serious disadvantage. And to avoid having you roll your eyes with skepticism, believing this to be a bunch of over-the-top hype, here are just a few of the results generated by strategies I'll be revealing to you:

a) An automotive business implemented one strategy that not only saved the business from possible bankruptcy, but also increased average sales from $120 up to $1,000 per customer. That's a 733% boost in revenue.

b) A retail store, making one small test to try a new approach, watched their sales increase up to 15% and the business triple in just three years as a result.

c) A plumbing firm implemented one strategy and caused the number of new inquiries to increase by 400%, with a 65% conversion rate to paying customers, in just seven months.

d) Using one simple strategy, a chiropractor took their business from $6,000 per month to $70,000 per month within 90 days. That translates into a 1066.667% increase in sales within just three months.

What kind of impact would results like these have in your life? Hopefully by now you realize your decision to read this book will be greatly beneficial for you, your family, and your business colleagues as you move forward.

DON'T FORGET YOUR FREE
BONUSES WORTH OVER $997

As my way of thanking you for your investment in this book, I will also be providing you with instructions to access additional FREE bonuses worth over $997 in value that I've created especially for you. These additional bonuses are to help you get even greater results from my techniques.

The access details will be revealed to you later in this book, at the appropriate time in your learning of the various strategies. Be sure to not skip any of the chapters or—even worse—fail to finish reading this book. These are bonuses you do not want to miss.

I want to ensure that you are as successful as possible as we move forward, so here are some tips to…

GET THE GREATEST RETURN
FOR YOUR INVESTMENT

1. Read through at least once. I created this book to be a fast, simple, and easy-to-read resource for the busy business owner or investor. As such, it's critical that you commit the time to finish reading the entire book within a short period of time to truly benefit from all the various ideas that will undoubtedly get your mind going as you progress through each chapter.

If, after reading just the first few chapters, you stop reading the book and just start implementing strategies—you'll still benefit— but you may get distracted with all the new ideas and fail to return to this book to benefit from the remaining strategies. Finish reading this entire book at least once before taking action.

2. Implement all the strategies. This book consists of ten chapters, nine of which comprise the series of marketing strategies and systems that should be implemented in any business you are considering to start or invest in, in order to maximize its profitability and minimize risks.

While the concepts in any one chapter have been proven to rapidly increase profits on their own, the synergistic effect and the exponential results generated by using them all together will make your business a juggernaut within its market.

3. Take action immediately. Along the same lines of ensuring this book would be an easy read, I also made sure to include three fast-action steps in each chapter for you to overcome any sort of procrastination in getting started. Speed of implementation is what separates a lot of the champion businesses from those that fade away.

I could have easily created 10 to 12 action steps for each section, but then that would probably cause you to delay getting started due to "lack of time" – thus the three simple steps. This should eliminate any excuses for not taking action immediately. Everyone wins.

I also want to ensure you are kept informed on any new updates to this book, success stories from other readers, as well as answers to any frequently asked questions coming in regarding the strategies or techniques mentioned in the various chapters.

RECEIVE FREE BOOK UPDATES AND TIPS BY REGISTERING YOUR EMAIL AT:
http://www.secrettoprofitableideas.com/freeupdates

This is just another way I could provide you with even more help and increase your successful results with my material.

But before we begin discussing the likelihood of your business ideas' profitability and success, there are five common mistakes that kill many businesses that you need to be aware of. In the next section, I'll share with you…

Chapter One:

The Five Fatal Business Traps

THIS INITIAL CHAPTER will help to ensure you have the best chance for success as you proceed forward with your business idea. As you already know, the majority of businesses will fail within the first two years. What you may not know, is that the reason for their failure is usually due to what I consider to be the five fatal mistakes.

In this chapter I will be explaining what I believe to be the five fatal mistakes are that you must avoid. I will also be giving you a glimpse into areas where very large corporations went wrong, and how even massive corporations can fall due to these mistakes. Knowing this information will help to prevent you from becoming financially and emotionally devastated as a result of these mistakes.

SOME ITEMS I COVER IN THIS CHAPTER:

a) Why building a business around your passion bankrupts many business owners

b) A $2.8 billion mistake and how you leverage it for your own gain

c) Why quitting your job to start a business can be a horrible idea

d) The three things a prospective customer must have before you try and sell to them

e) Why offering customers low prices is a guaranteed way to go out of business

Now that you have a sample of what's to come, let's get started with…

TRAP #1 - FOLLOW YOUR PASSION

Entrepreneurs often approach me stating that they have "*a really great idea*" for a business. Our typical conversation usually starts off with them saying how they're really passionate about a certain industry, topic, cause, etc. and that they *believe* that they have a great idea that will make a "*ton of money*."

Why would following their passion be considered a mistake? Because they are getting too excited about something without having first validated that it's a profitable idea. Being good in theory does not always equate to being profitable in reality. Many entrepreneurs have started up businesses and invested a ton of time and money into them, only to embarrassingly realize after the fact that not enough people cared to spend any money on their "*awesome idea*."

What about existing businesses? Surely if you expand on a current product line with a new idea, it can't be as bad, *right*? Wrong.

For example, are you familiar with the Ford Motor Company? If you're not, Ford is an American multinational automobile manufacturer that currently generates billions and billions in revenue each year. And they are just as guilty of having fallen into this trap as the Average Joe business owner.

Why do I say that?

AN EMBARRASSING $2.8 BILLION MISTAKE

Well from 1958 to 1960, Ford manufactured a full-size car known as the Edsel. This was a vehicle Ford *expected* to make significant inroads into the market share of both General Motors and Chrysler (competing automobile companies). Unfortunately, contrary to Ford's internal plans and projections, the Edsel never gained popularity with American car buyers. It sold poorly – very poorly.

What was the end result for Ford?

Ford Motor Company had lost $350 million on the Edsel's development, manufacturing and marketing by the end of 1960. This is approximately the equivalent of $2,831,563,927 in 2014 dollars. Ford *thought* they were creating an amazing product based on their *own* beliefs of what the market wanted, but not based within the reality of what the market demonstrated they actually wanted to buy at that time.

What should you take away from this example?

Primarily that even a big company, employing hundreds of individuals with fancy business degrees, can make costly (multibillion-dollar) mistakes, and that you should not base your decision of what's a *"good idea"* solely on an assumption related to what you're passionate about.

Does this mean you can't use what you're passionate about as the starting point for a profitable idea? Of course not! But it does have to be done properly, which we'll talk about more in Chapter 2: Find the Flaws.

However, right now, let's address the second trap which is...

TRAP #2 - CREATING A JOB

The second fatal mistake many business owners make is wanting to escape their *"awful job"* by just starting their own business. After all, by being their own boss they will have the freedom and control they dreamed of, right? Not so fast.

What tends to happen, and which you may have experienced yourself, is the business owner ends up creating a business that consumes all of their time and energy. Essentially they trade one job for an even more demanding and stressful position, but this time it's within their own company.

This type of situation leads to financial, relationship, and even mental challenges as your business begins to grow and further increases the demand on your time and resources. It's a never-ending cycle that eventually leads to the business disastrously imploding.

Now when a business is just starting out, it's common for the business owner to be all positions required to make it successful, but it's very, very critical that an exit strategy is in place to allow the business owner to step away from the business, yet it's still able to generate a profitable income.

THIS IS WHAT YOUR BUSINESS NEEDS
FOR LONG-TERM SUCCESS...

Your business needs to be able to generate *passive income*, that is, without your presence being required in order for it to make sales, produce and deliver the product or services to customers, and promote the company to your target market of prospects. If this is not the case, then as in a typical fatal business trap fashion, it's only a matter of time before the business will fade away, which is typically around the same time you do, whether physically or mentally.

I will expand on how to implement systems along with your business idea to allow it to scale and grow, while reducing the work required, in Chapter 6: The Five Crucial Systems to Implement.

The main thing to take away from this trap is that you must not feel like you have to go at implementing your profitable idea alone. What do I mean when I refer to going at it alone? Well, reaching out and tapping into an existing network of business-minded individuals is a great start. If one doesn't exist that suits your needs, create it. Being able to bounce ideas, frustrations, and successes off of an effective mastermind group will be very valuable to you in the long run.

Just remember: passive income is key. Any business idea that you come up with must be designed to allow it to operate without you — structured to do so from the start. This allows you to continue to generate idea, after idea, after idea, without burning yourself (and your resources) out.

Since we're on the topic of avoiding burning out resources, let's talk about the next common mistake which many businesses owners fall into the trap of making...

TRAP #3 - TRYING TO APPEAL TO EVERYONE

This is the business trap that just seems to make sense for a business to do...until you realize you shouldn't have done it. Unfortunately, by the time you realize how devastating a mistake it is to try and make your business idea appeal to "everyone," you will have burned through a massive amount of time, money, and energy.

How do so many business owners fall in to this trap? Usually it occurs right from the start due to the height of emotional excitement over their own idea(s).

When I ask these business owners who their target market is, I often receive a response of *"everyone!"* or some very large and generic demographic description. An example of this would be a description like *"all males over the age of 18,"* etc. There are three glaring issues with this line of thinking:

The first problem is that small businesses do not have unlimited money to spend on marketing and relationship building. Which means if your business is trying to target a demographic which is (using the previous example of all adult males) nearly half the planet, you will probably go broke even trying.

WHY MUST YOU THINK SMALL TO GROW BIG?

The important thing for a new or existing small business to do is to make every dollar count. This means targeting a much more focused and smaller target market that you can receive the highest return on investment from.

The second problem is that typically business owners who fall for this trap are not describing qualified prospects. They are actually describing potential suspects – people they suspect *might* have an interest in what they have to offer, but actually haven't made any overt action to verify they actually would ever spend money to obtain the solution being offered.

And finally, the third problem is that simply trying to appeal to those who are interested isn't enough. Heck, I'm interested in owning a sports team someday, but that isn't enough. Your business must focus on appealing to those who are interested and are *capable* of buying. Otherwise, you will be burning through tons of resources for very little return, until eventually you are so far gone there's no coming back.

THERE ARE ONLY THREE THINGS TO WATCH FOR

Remember, keep it focused and target only qualified prospects: those who have shown they have a capability, interest, and need for what you have to offer them. *I will expand more on that need in Chapter 2: Find the Flaws.*

Fortunately for your business, many of your competitors will not be as educated about this fact. Actually, start taking a look around at the marketing materials used by other businesses and you will probably notice that many of them are using very generic messages with no clear target market. Use this to your advantage.

In fact, if your competitors are foolish enough to try and appeal to everyone, they are most definitely already deep into the ticking time bomb which is…

TRAP #4 - A "ME TOO" MENTALITY

Chances are you will fall into this trap, if you haven't yet already. Many business owners, just as they are starting out, tend to take a look at what everyone else in the industry seems to be doing to generate sales and stay in business. Then they follow suit.

Essentially, these business owners will try and get their business to *"fit in"* with what has typically been done within the industry – from products and services, marketing methods and prices, to retail space setup and even how they operate.

Why does this happen? The thought process tends to revolve around the fact that these existing businesses have been around much longer, so they must know what they're doing. The new business owners then think to themselves that they will just do what these older companies are doing, but they'll try and do it better.

YOU MUST STOP THE INCEST

These business owners will then try and make minor incremental improvements to the way they run their business, but for the most part they will still stay within the *"comfort zone"* that the industry is used to. The problem with this thinking is that it leads to a sort of marketing incest. Everyone just keeps looking at what everyone else within the industry is doing, but nobody is really breaking out and thinking outside the box for ideas.

Apple Inc. is a multinational corporation that went from the brink of business death in the 90s to becoming one of the most powerful and influential brands in the world… by thinking outside of the box, by being innovative.

Apple has consistently chosen to push the limits of their customer service, product development, and corporate environment, leaving behind other businesses that had previously been successful for decades. Their competitors had survived for so long mainly by making small improvements on competing devices within the industry, but not really standing out. Apple has now left most of these other companies scrambling to even remain in business. As I mentioned previously, such a fate can happen to any business, big or small, that falls into any of these fatal traps.

One of the biggest mistakes some aspiring business owners make is practically copying the products and services of a competing business, but only trying to differentiate themselves in their marketing by promoting themselves as "the lowest price option." This is definitely one of the worst "me too" mistakes that can be made.

OFFERING LOW PRICES IS BUSINESS SUICIDE

The hard reality for these types of businesses is that trying to compete based only on having the lowest price offer is a recipe for disaster. It essentially becomes a race to the bottom, as only one business can truly be "the lowest priced" option. This leads to added pressure on that business to survive on razor-thin profit margins, forcing them to make cuts to many business areas just to stay afloat.

As wages for staff can't remain competitive for quality work, customer service declines. Maintenance costs end up being directed to the lowest bidder and the quality of their work is reflected in that price. All this will eventually lead to customers going elsewhere and the businesses reputation spiralling downwards.

In fact, history is riddled with businesses that at one time or another were massively successful due to having the lowest prices… until someone came along who could go even lower. The end result: Those businesses eventually faded away.

Even retail giants like Wal-Mart are feeling the pressure from Internet-based competitors such as Amazon that have the infrastructure in place to offer large discounts on products without the massive overhead that their retail counterparts have. Unfortunately, it's hard to recover from this pricing mistake as any customers they have built up are only retained due to the low prices, so once a lower price option is found, these customers leave.

By having the only distinguishable difference between your business and a competing business be the fact you have lower prices, you are slowly going to tighten the noose around the neck of your business.

There are ways to use low prices for short-term offers to generate new customers, but it has to be done correctly or it will do more harm than good. I don't want to dwell on pricing too much; we'll save pricing strategies as a topic for another day.

The main thing to remember is that it is high profit margins that will give power to your business to provide more value to customers, and execute more comprehensive marketing strategies to obtain new customers. It is also a make-or-break factor for many potential investors as well.

IF YOU'RE BORING YOU WILL BE BROKE

Realtors, accountants, lawyers and a plethora of other service and sales professionals are among many industries where the "me too" mentality runs rampant. They fall into the trap of doing nothing to show their target market what sets them apart from their competition, and just hoping they are selected by a client or customer who happens to come across them.

However, the fact that any of your competitors have fallen into this "me too" trap opens up even more profitable opportunities for your business once you understand and implement the powerful strategies I reveal in Chapter 2: Find the Flaws.

How can you avoid this costly trap completely? *I will reveal the secret in detail within Chapter 3: The Secret Unveiled.* For now the main thing you must do is to always question the way everything is done within your industry, even if it's been a standard forever.

You must verify why things are being done the way they are. Seek empirical proof that it is truly the best way. Do not just go along with the belief it should be done because "that's the way it has always been done."

The lack of willingness to challenge the status quo is actually what leads many businesses into...

TRAP #5 - FAILURE TO ADAPT

The need to adapt is not just a requirement for business; it's a requirement for the survival of any living thing that exists. In fact, Charles Darwin summed up how you need to view your business with the one quote: "It is not the strongest of the species that survive, nor the most intelligent, but the one most responsive to change."

Where many successful, multimillion-dollar businesses eventually fail is in this trap. I cannot emphasize this enough, but you are never too big to fail. Remember this.

However, also take comfort in the fact that even the largest million-dollar corporations can be wiped out. Why? Because it means that even if you are competing in an industry with large businesses, with the secret I share with you in Chapter 3: The Secret Unveiled, combined with the other strategies in this book, you can still topple them like David taking out Goliath.

In my study of what makes businesses successful, I noticed that what allowed small businesses with profitable ideas to eventually destroy their larger "untouchable" competitors was the latter's failure to adapt. In fact, you have already seen examples of this throughout recent years.

FROM FORTUNE 500 TO FAILURE

Take the Eastman Kodak Company for example. The Eastman Kodak Company, better known as Kodak, is an American technology company best known for its photographic film products. Founded in 1888 by George Eastman, Kodak was the "untouchable" beast in the industry; in fact, in 1976 it held 90% market share of the photographic film sales within the entire United States of America.

The fact Kodak had 90% market share, with profits peaking at nearly $16 billion in annual revenue, and the fact they had dominated their industry for well over 100 years, caused Kodak to feel it had nothing to fear. So when Steve Sasson, the Kodak engineer who invented the first digital camera in 1975, approached management with the idea, management brushed it off and killed the project. After all, nothing could possibly replace film, their bread and butter.

Almost forty years later, in January 2012, Kodak filed for Chapter 11 bankruptcy protection. The mighty had fallen. Kodak had failed to adapt, failed to respond to the desires of their market.

Perhaps you remember a little American company by the name of Blockbuster Entertainment Inc.? Founded in 1985, here was another goliath in the corporate world, but this time in the entertainment industry. At its peak in 2004, Blockbuster had up to 60,000 employees and more than 9,000 stores. It was spending millions and millions of dollars annually on "hilarious" Super

Bowl commercials to brand the company even more. Yep, branded them right into oblivion.

Blockbuster failed to adapt to the needs of their market as well. They failed to transition to the more convenient direct-to-your-door type of services that newcomer Netflix and Redbox offered their customer base. Despite having critically acclaimed commercials and advertisements, Blockbuster eventually filed for bankruptcy on September 23, 2010.

Interestingly enough, back in the year 2000, Blockbuster had the chance to purchase a still fledgling Netflix for $50 million. Just like Kodak, they thought they were going to remain unbeatable forever. Instead, their corporate mentality and slow adaptation capability caused them to share the same fate.

HOW TO TELL AN IDEA IS A GAME CHANGER

You will notice more and more larger corporations buying up smaller companies who have stumbled across innovative new solutions to provide the market. What better way to stay ahead of the innovation curve of potential new competitors. After all, because consumers are constantly on the lookout for what could be the next hot thing in the market, large corporations must remain more vigilant than ever to show they are coming out with new products and solutions, even if it means buying up the companies that actually developed them.

Heck, you could even look within your own pocket to see the speed at which adaptation can happen. Do you own a smartphone? Then you are witness to how fast the demands of the market are changing on an annual basis. Research In Motion Ltd. (RIM), a Canadian telecommunication and wireless equipment company best known as the developer of the BlackBerry brand of smartphones, learned this the hard way.

RIM was formed in 1984 and was for a long time considered the dominant innovative company in the smartphone market for business and government usage. In 2010, RIM was reportedly in command of over 43% of the US market share for business and government usage of phone devices. However, just a few short years later in 2013, that market share plummeted to 3.8% due to competition from Apple's new iPhone devices and Google's Android brands. RIM thought they had the market locked down. Innovative new solutions quickly proved that not to be the case.

I could continue on with dozens and dozens of similar examples, multiple stories of large corporations that had generated many millions of dollars a year and had been around for decades, companies that felt their sales and market position were untouchable… only to be proven wrong.

And this is not limited to just companies which sell physical products in a retail style format. Service industries must be even more competitive on how they adapt to the wishes of their market before their competitors do.

Speed of implementation is critical. Kodak and Blockbuster, for example, eventually did try and offer similar products and solutions that competitors had gained their market share with, but it was too little too late.

The point remains simple and clear. You must be constantly aware of—and quickly adapt to—the needs of your market, or you open the door to someone else to take your market share from you.

YOUR 3-STEP ACTION PLAN FOR CHAPTER ONE:

1. Think like an investor. Ensure you are focusing constantly on the return on investment you will get for every action you take.

This includes the idea itself. You should know if and when it should be profitable before you even get started. If you don't know these things, don't take any further action until you do. Executing a business idea just because you think it will work, or want the "freedom" of being a business owner, does not make it a worthwhile venture. In fact, it could leave you financially devastated if you aren't careful.

2. Remain self-aware. Constantly assess where your ideas, and your business as a whole, are in relation to these five traps. It's easy to become complacent and over-confident should things be going smoothly for your business, but remember: the bigger you are, the harder you will fall. It's not enough to just be "open to change"; you must be willing to leave your current comfort zone to remain competitive. Failure to avoid these traps consistently just opens the door to the same graveyard containing other businesses that have missed the mark as well.

3. Watch your competitors. Not just in terms of how they run their business and how they implement marketing strategies, but watch for how competitors have fallen into these fatal traps. Capitalize on this. Use the opportunity to dominate them within your industry to capture as much market share as possible. No business is immune from being beaten, especially if they have fallen into these traps. They will eventually succumb to the right competitor with the right profitable idea. Remember this.

Now that we have gone over the fatal mistakes you must avoid on your quest for a profitable business idea, you may be wondering how to find sources for profitable business ideas.

We cover that next in…

Chapter Two:
Find the Flaws

FINDING THE FLAWS within a market is the first, and probably the most critical, aspect in your journey to discovering and implementing a profitable business idea.

After finishing this chapter, you will learn why most businesses fail in their development of new products and solutions. You will also be able to prevent large losses of your own resources in terms of wasted time, money, and energy.

In the previous chapter, I mentioned that two of the five fatal traps business owners make when pursing a new business idea are following their passion and failing to adapt to changes in the market. By utilizing the information in this chapter, you will be able to identify profitable business ideas within an area you are passionate about and have actual data to back up why it's a profitable idea, as opposed to just what you feel is a good idea.

You will also be able to continuously identify new opportunities and needs within your market for your business to develop solutions for.

SOME ITEMS I COVER IN THIS CHAPTER:

a) Why your friends and family may do more harm than good in regards to your business ideas

b) A common mistake entrepreneurs make when identifying a market segment to target

c) What motivates your potential buyers the most, and how to profitably harness it

d) The only action required to uncover unlimited profitable opportunities

e) The most expensive mistake even multimillion-dollar corporations make and how to easily avoid it

Let's get started.

There's an old saying, "build it and they will come." This is great advice...for disappointment. Instead, I prefer this saying: *"Find out what the market wants, and give it to them."*

Why? Because it gets to the root of what this entire chapter is about. The first quote is more closely associated with Trap #1: Follow Your Passion. It suggests that if you believe in something, just go for it, and the market will come to you. Big mistake!

HOW TO ENSURE YOUR IDEA SELLS

It is more profitable and less risky to avoid assuming what the market will respond to, and instead to just give them exactly what they say they want to begin with. This is what the second saying means. This is what finding the flaws within a market is all about.

Many aspiring entrepreneurs tend to try and promote what they want to sell, and not what the market wants to buy.

You can either think like your prospects think, or you can try and get your prospects to see their world as you see it. Guess which group tends to quickly join the 80% of businesses that fail. It's all about supply versus demand – Marketing 101. Your ideas must stem from preexisting demand. Do not gamble your resources by hoping to create substantial demand for a supply you decided to create.

Market research is one area that has to be done correctly; otherwise, your business will begin producing and providing products and services that fail... horribly.

Do you know a business colleague who was excited about a new product or service they were launching, and confident it would do well, only to watch their dreams of massive sales go down in flames? This is a prime example of someone who did not do proper market research ahead of time.

When I refer to market research and finding the flaws in the market, I am talking about getting your information from those who actually will purchase your products and services.

DON'T MAKE THIS PERSONAL

Unfortunately, many business owners have been led astray by choosing to rely on close friends and family for their thoughts when it comes to business ideas. Their opinions do not count as valid research or realistic prediction of demand from your market. You must get your feedback from the only people that count: those who vote with their money.

When you ask people close to you if they think something is a good idea, or if it will "*work*," it's easy for them to either agree with you or provide feedback of what they think they would buy from you. Many will just tell you what they believe you want to hear, especially if they don't want to put a damper on your excitement over your "great new idea."

However, unless they will be buying your product or service, a person's feedback doesn't help you much when it comes to how your actual target market will respond.

Another error entrepreneurs make when identifying a target market is collecting feedback from the wrong groups. You must not only ensure your target market is *willing* to give you sizable sums of money for the products and services they are looking for, but that they are also *able* to give you sizable sums of money. It's common for large groups to say how much they wish a certain solution existed, but even if it did, they couldn't afford to actually obtain it.

WHAT IS YOUR PROBLEM?

It is also important to realize that the target market should actually be a problem or burning desire, and not a demographic of individuals. For example, you could be looking to do market research regarding current flaws regarding gardening products for eliminating weeds.

Typically, most business owners would then try and say they are targeting a demographic consisting of females, between 30 and 60 years of age, that own a house, etc. Instead, because you are to target the problem itself, your target market is anyone who has issues or comments regarding the elimination of weeds from their property. This group would consist of pet owners afraid of harsh chemicals, people with chemical allergies, those with environmental concerns, etc. From there, you could drill down to more specific niche groups if you want.

The Scotts Miracle-Gro Company is a great example of a company that has been using this concept. Founded in 1868, this American multinational company began with Orlando M. Scott selling premium lawn seed to homeowners, and today generates over $2.82 billion in annual revenues and has offices and research facilities worldwide.

When you get a chance, take a look at their product lineup of Scotts solutions for a variety of specific lawn problems based on the demands of the market. Their growth since 1868 up to now is definitely a great example of what a successful business does right, in terms of adapting to market needs and proper market research.

SUCCESSFUL COMPANIES ARE
ALWAYS DOING THIS:

Being able to find the gap within the solutions being provided to the market will open many profitable opportunities for the aspiring entrepreneur. Look for the pending subdivision potential of a currently hot market and target it with a solution made especially for them. For example: music events, the entertainment industry, nutrition, fitness etc.

Just take a look at all the different types of athletic shoes that exist: tennis, basketball, soccer, etc. and the many features and benefits each claims to give the user. Running shoes are very similar, but shoes for sprinters, compared to shoes for marathon runners, compared to shoes for a basketball player, etc. will appear differently in the eyes of the market. They are looking for solutions that seem to speak to their specific needs.

Heck, take a walk down the household product aisle at a grocery store and take a gander at the various kitchen cleaning, bathroom sanitizing, laundry washing products, etc. As I said, the riches are in the niches.

This way you are able to target a customer group you want to work with. You can avoid the trap of coming up with a business idea just based on your passion, and instead pick a market you are passionate about to develop a business idea for. It just requires a change of your perspective.

ONLY TWO THINGS WILL MOTIVATE YOUR MARKET TO BUY

When doing your research, it is important to remember that people are basically motivated by only two things: *gaining pleasure and avoiding pain*. Identify what the primary motivators for your market are, based on these two things. What comments or suggestions do they have for what would bring them more pleasure in regards to a business idea? What pains and frustrations do they currently have that they would like removed?

In fact, before picking your target market, make sure you determine if they are clearly mentioning any pain, urgency, embarrassment, or irrational passions regarding their situation. Do they feel a strong emotion? Find what motivates them at a level deeper than a simple desire. Identify the biggest challenge or obstacle in their path that affects them emotionally, and provide a solution for it.

You can't motivate others to want something they don't already want. You can't create motivation, no matter how persuasive you think you are. It must already be there, inside your prospect. If not, you're wasting your time and appealing to the wrong audience, which is making your job of selling so much more difficult.

Everyone is already motivated. The only question is, *"by what?"*

YOU MUST LISTEN FOR THIS

This is why the amount of potential profitable opportunities you uncover is directly related to asking enough of the right questions from your target market. The better investigating you do as to what it is they really want—and don't want—the more profitable solutions you can develop to offer them.

Also keep in mind that profitable possibilities are everywhere. For example, take a look at your own career / profession and the problems you encounter at work that cause your staff or co-workers to gripe and complain. Software, tools, service providers, etc., any of these areas may require better solutions.

There's a Canadian company, the Setcan® Corporation, which was established in 2006 along similar logic. Due to the owner's experience within law enforcement, he realized there was a lack of reality-based training products for law enforcement purposes. Now, the company is the world's largest provider of reality-based training equipment and instructor level certifications for law enforcement, military, corrections and security agencies. They targeted a problem, not a demographic.

As you can see, it's not complicated. You don't need to be a "genius." It's just a matter of finding out what people want and showing them how to get it. Determine their problem and show them how to solve it. Identify their current frustrations with the current solutions they are using, or the objections they have for not even wanting to purchase them at all.

THIS IS HOW YOU CAN PROFIT
WHILE COMPETITORS STRUGGLE

Keep up to date with new demands they may have as their own circumstances and situations change, and what needs they have that are not currently being met. Then fill those demands and needs.

The McDonald's restaurant chain is a great example of a large corporation that adapted to the demands of their market after finding flaws within their market. In the 1970s McDonalds observed that the American public was on-the-go more than ever, and fast service of food was a priority. They did some market research and determined that a quick breakfast would be welcomed by consumers.

In 1972 the company pioneered breakfast fast food with the introduction of the Egg McMuffin. It was a huge success. Five years later, McDonald's added a full breakfast line to their menu, and by 1987, one-fourth of all breakfasts eaten out in the United States came from McDonald's restaurants.

This is a company that could have stuck with what they had been known for, making hamburgers, but instead expanded out of their comfort zone, adapted to the needs of the market, and dominated the fast food industry globally as a result.

WHAT BUSINESS ARE YOU IN?

A successful business owner realizes they are not in the business of what they sell—they are in the marketing business, providing solutions to what their market wants; for example, the business owner that believes they are only in the jewelry business versus the entrepreneur who adds online commerce, jewelry courses etc. to their solution offering.

When it comes to searching for flaws within a market, you don't need to create a solution from scratch—one that has never before been seen—in fact this is probably the most expensive and time-consuming approach. Instead, improve upon a product or service that already exists, one that your market is already familiar with, one that has already proven to be profitable.

Pick a market or industry that already exists and has solutions being offered that are being bought already. If you have to educate the market as to why they need your solution, which they have never seen anything like it before, you're venturing down a road that is expensive and extremely risky. Ensure you are selecting a target market that is already actively looking for a solution. To further enhance the profitability of your idea, select a market that also believes they have few or no desirable solutions currently available.

YOUR 3-STEP ACTION PLAN FOR CHAPTER TWO:

1. Find a problem to solve. Identify the market you will target by determining a group with a problem you want to solve with your business idea. The more people affected by a common problem, the more potential exists to profit from your solution. It's all about supply and demand.

2. Ensure the market is profitable. It is not enough to just locate a group with a problem. You must also ensure the group is actively searching for a solution to their problem, and have both the desire and capability to spend money to obtain it. Also confirm that there is already a solution(s) being offered and being bought by the market, but that the market is not entirely satisfied with.

3. Ask the right questions. Your primary goal is to find the flaws within the current solutions being offered to the market, and then provide them with a more desirable one. In order to do this, you must solicit feedback from your prospects. The easiest way to accomplish this would be through the use of a survey which can be completed online or in paper form within your business.

Another option is to simply frequent message boards, forums, blogs, and websites used by your target market and read over the reviews, criticisms, etc. that the market is writing about these competing solutions.

Now that you have determined what the market's wants and needs are, it is time to reveal the secret behind profitable business ideas that deliver solutions to a target market's problems.

At long last, it is time for...

Chapter Three:
The Secret Unveiled

IN THIS CHAPTER, I finally reveal the secret to profitable business ideas. However, you may have noticed that there are a total of ten chapters in this book, which means while the secret will ensure you have the competitive upper hand in your industry, there is still much to be done behind the scenes to make you truly unbeatable. An idea on its own is a great start, but not enough. Several things will have to combine to make your idea wildly profitable.

When you use the information in this chapter, you will be able to truly determine if a business idea will be profitable right from the very start. Whether you are looking to start up a business, expand your business' solutions, or invest in a profitable business idea, this information will help you filter out what's worth your time and what is not.

SOME ITEMS I COVER IN THIS CHAPTER:

a) The two most important questions you will ever answer in your business

b) The $58.5 billion secret to investing in profitable businesses

c) Some of the key factors behind the massive success of the iPod, iPad and iPhone devices

d) A profitable tactic to keep in mind the next time you drive through a drive-through

e) How to build an army of passionate buyers that actively support you

Now let's finally get to what you've been waiting for.

First thing's first, let me explain what the secret to profitable ideas actually is. The concept is simple, but it is actually made up of three parts.

The first part of the secret is having a product or service that offers a clear and unique advantage over your competition. It seems like this would be common-sense economics, but surprisingly most businesses do not do this, or they may think they are offering an advantage which isn't really considered a superior advantage in the eyes of their market at all.

THE QUESTION TO ASK YOURSELF
BEFORE YOU DO ANYTHING

You must be able to provide an appealing answer to the question, *"why should I choose your solution over every other option being made available to me, including doing nothing at all?"* The reality is that without a unique advantage, you're just a commodity in the eyes of your market.

If you're not offering any sort of advantage over competing solutions, your business will be surviving based solely on your target market finding your prices acceptable, or your location convenient to access, etc. However, you will be crushed by any competing business—possibly utilizing this very book—that offers your market something appealing that you do not.

The second part of the three components which make up the secret is the second question you must ask. *"What is it about your idea that would prevent a competitor from simply copying your idea once it has proved to be profitable?"*

They key aspect of your unique advantage is that it must not be easily copied. If it can be copied and offered by competitors, then you will no longer have a unique advantage in your market.

BUILD AN ELECTRIC FENCE
AROUND YOUR MARKET

Warren Buffet, an American widely considered to be the most successful investor of the 20th century, with over $58.5 billion in personal net worth, is regarded as a master at choosing good businesses. When asked how he selects the businesses he buys stock in, Buffet stated, *"Good businesses are in some way reasonably sheltered from competition."* In essence, what Warren is speaking to is having a profound, clear, compelling and sustainable differentiation.

In a recent issue of Inc. Magazine, Ann Hand, CEO of Project Frog, a San Francisco-based company that builds energy-efficient prefab buildings, stated, "Not much has changed in the construction industry in the past 100 years or so … it's an industry just waiting to be disrupted." It seems her company is doing exactly that.

By using standardized core components and less-expensive materials, Project Frog can produce buildings in half the time and at 20% of the cost of traditional construction. Not only that, a Project Frog building consumes half the energy of a conventional structure. This unique advantage that Project Frog is able to provide in a market full of generic competitors has helped it land more than $40 million in funding from investors, and generate over $28.7 million in revenue in 2012.

CAN YOU DO BETTER?

Dyson Ltd. is another prime example of consistently profitable business ideas as a result of clearly unique advantages in their products. Dyson is a British technology company that designs and manufactures vacuum cleaners, hand dryers, bladeless fans, and heaters. The company prides itself in its engineering products which work in different and better ways than their predecessors.

Actually, Dyson's founder, James Dyson, created 5,127 prototypes of his first machine, a household vacuum cleaner that functioned without the need for costly dirt collection bags. Interestingly enough, similar to the Kodak example from chapter one, Dyson approached manufacturing companies like Hoover to license his machine. He was rejected. The big manufacturers did not want to license the design because the vacuum bag market was worth $500 million to them. Dyson's idea was a threat to their profits.

Unfortunately for the greedy manufacturers, Dyson's idea was extremely advantageous in the eyes of the market. Dyson Ltd. is now generating $6 billion in annual revenues. Hoover attempted to copy Dyson's designs once they proved successful, but in the year 1999 ended up being found guilty of patent infringement.

When your target market is initially presented with your business idea or marketing pitch, the first thing someone will think —subconsciously or consciously—is *"how will this benefit me in a superior way, compared with every other product making pitches for my business?"* This is especially true in your printed messages or commercials utilizing television, radio, social media, etc.

YOUR ADVANTAGE OVER COMPETITORS

Your unique advantage may be in providing the market with a solution that makes obtaining the desired result they are looking for easier, faster, or cheaper.

For example, Dana Gleason, the founder of Mystery Ranch, a company that designs backpacks for skiers and mountaineers, discovered his niche after he was approached by a customer who happened to also be a Navy SEAL. This customer persuaded Gleason to design a backpack specifically for military usage. That first prototype led to a contract with the SEALs, followed by a host of other Pentagon contracts. The main advantage of these backpacks that won over the military was the fact they helped the wearer carry heavy loads with as little strain on the body as possible. The frame was specifically designed to support unusually shaped and unbalanced loads like large weapons and equipment.

This is also what caused the downfall of the Eastman Kodak Company, as I mentioned previously. The creation of digital photography brought with it the advantage of photographs being viewable instantly without the need to wait for the film to be developed. It also was a much cheaper solution compared to the recurring costs of purchasing film.

The same could be said about James Dyson's bag-less vacuum idea. It allowed the market to forgo the expensive recurring cost of additional bags, and still achieve the same—if not better—result. Dyson provided a unique advantage that was easier and cheaper for the market compared to the solutions they were previously being offered.

YOUR UNBELIEVABLE EXPERIENCE

The advantage you offer may not need to apply to a specific result. Your advantage may simply be more appealing due to the experience your solution provides the user while they obtain the result they're looking for. This could happen in the form of providing a one-stop shop solution for customers to avoid having to deal with multiple providers. It could also be a higher quality user experience, similar to what Apple Inc. offers users of their products.

When Cineplex Inc., a Canadian company mainly known for its expansive chain of movie theatre locations, realized the growing competition they were up against from their market preferring to stay at home to watch movies, they did some research. The end result was changes made to the movie watching experience in their theatres. Larger screens, better sound, motion-capable seats that were synched to the story of the movie, the ability to reserve seats in advance to avoid having to wait in long lines for seats, V.I.P. theatres with comfortable seats along with alcohol and food service, etc. Cineplex offers their market a unique movie-going experience they can't replicate at home.

THE UNDENIABLE VALUE PROVIDED

Perhaps you offer a unique value advantage. The Walt Disney Company was a pioneer in the theme park world when it offered the market the ability to pay one price and be able to get in all the rides all day long. This was an advantage over the traditional method of purchasing tickets to be used at each individual ride within the park.

We can even relate back to a previous example in this book, Netflix. Netflix was considered to be the "Blockbuster Killer," practically eliminating the video rental market as it did away with the traditional approach. Netflix offered customers the ability to access unlimited movies for a fixed rate of a few dollars per month – no need to leave their homes in cold weather, no additional late fees for forgotten videos that weren't returned on time. Nowadays there are many companies offering what Netflix did initially, but for a limited time it dominated the market with a unique value advantage.

DO YOU PUT YOUR MARKET AT EASE?

Or perhaps your advantage is one of providing peace of mind to the market should they be unhappy with your new idea. Providing extended warrants and return periods on new products and services is a prime example of this. Bed Bath and Beyond Inc. is well known for their incredible return policy: if at any time you are unhappy with your purchase, simply bring it back for a refund – doesn't matter if it's been ten days, ten months, or ten years. They have been extremely profitable as a result of this peace of mind they offer their market.

It is very important that you also don't just expect your market to figure out how your idea can be used to improve their situation or what makes it different. *You must clearly tell them what advantages you offer* so they can imagine benefiting from the advantages your idea will provide over what they have previously been offered.

This can be easily done by sharing an example of what their life was like before your solution, and then comparing that to how things will be after benefiting from your solution in terms of accomplishing the same results compared to other options. Perhaps you can simply explain how your idea will reduce their amount of work, time, or money required to achieve results versus the current way they are doing things, etc.

No matter what advantage you ensure your idea has, it is absolutely vital you build a moat around your advantage and your market. Your idea must not be easily stolen or copied; otherwise, it will not be able to remain competitive in the long run. Warren Buffet only invests in companies with built-in moats to keep out copycat competitors who will try and steal market share. Find a way to prevent this.

This can be accomplished via exclusive access to production resources, industry partnerships, patents, delivery methods – heck, even restaurants utilize "secret ingredients," etc. This is another reason why patent lawsuits and corporate spying is prevalent in this day and age. Everyone is trying to discover the secret behind their competitor's advantages, while guarding their own.

"I'LL BELIEVE IT WHEN I SEE IT!"

It's not enough to just claim your idea or solution offers an advantage to the market. We live in a society of skepticism and resistance to big promises. You will require proof of your advantages. You must be able to demonstrate and explain what makes your business idea so much better. Without belief, nobody buys. This is why demonstrating claims, such as through video advertisements like informercials, is so vital.

The power of a good demonstration can be seen with Steve Jobs' introduction of Apple's revolutionary new iPod and iPhone debut presentations. It wasn't enough to just claim how the products would be better; Jobs had to demonstrate it. A solid demonstration allows your solution to become real in the eyes of your market. It allows your prospect to imagine using it in their current situation and actually benefiting from it.

Remember, in Chapter 2: Find the Flaws, it is important that you identify the main objections or complaints your market has.

With that information in hand, you must now ensure your new idea or solution addresses and solves these issues. You will then be able to easily attract those who want to buy a solution for their needs but didn't, because of their concerns regarding existing solutions not being addressed or resolved.

The great thing about utilizing unique advantages in your positioning of a product or service is that it can also apply to your ability to appeal to others in other ways. A unique advantage can be used to attract and retain employees for your business. Money alone is not always enough of an incentive to attract great talent.

The same principle can apply to someone working to secure a full-time career in a field of their choice. Showcasing their unique advantage over competing applicants with their cover letters may quickly tip the scale in their favour. A unique advantage may also keep that person from being laid off or their job outsourced to someone willing to do it for much cheaper. Once again, it's about positioning themselves to be irreplaceable and not just a commodity.

Your work doesn't end with one advantage though, not by a long shot. You need to be constantly searching to identify ways to make your product more exclusive, unique, or rare. This doesn't mean you need to be extra creative or innovative, but it does mean you need to keep an eye out for ideas in other industries and market which you could implement within your own.

ALWAYS THINK OUTSIDE THE BOX

For example, fast food restaurants with drive-through service are commonly observed around the world, but did you know the idea was first implemented in 1928 for City Center Bank? Now other industries are using that "innovative idea" but applying it to their own market's needs. Pharmacies, postal service, grocery stores, liquor stores, and even a marriage chapel in Las Vegas! Look for sources of ideas everywhere which may not be new to the world but may be new to your own market.

Another profitable benefit of utilizing this secret, and implanting unique advantages into your idea, is that you may be able to charge higher prices than your competitors while still attracting more new leads and paying customers. Since you will be the only one who is able to provide the solution you provide, the way you provide it, you don't have to worry about competitors undercutting you. Your competition will be left scratching their heads and watching with envy as you swallow up their market share.

Just look at how Apple's iPad computer tablets have dominated the market right up until the time this book was published. Due to the high-quality user experience that Apple ensures its products possess, its iPad line has the highest satisfaction rating three years running despite influx in low-cost options. Competing tablets try and draw customers with low prices, but the market has shown it wants the unique experience only the iPad provides due to its patented technology. Pay attention to how many times Apple executives refer to "the experience" of using any of their products during their presentations.

The third and final component of the secret to profitable business ideas is the need to have a bigger purpose or goal behind your idea. Introducing a business idea for the sake of it can work will not be nearly as powerful as when it is attached to a vision or mission.

BUILDING YOUR ARMY OF PASSIONATE BUYERS

Your business must have a mission, a purpose to do more than just make money from the market. Identify the bad guy you will champion against on behalf of your market, and allow them to passionately rally around your cause.

Apple's unofficial mission is to be the leader in innovation, to make the best products which are not only beautiful but also simplify the way things are currently being done to make for a better quality user experience. As a result, Apple has a passionate market following that fully believes in the company and its products.

Walter Elias Disney, co-founder of The Walt Disney Company, said he was "in the business of selling happiness." In fact he believed in selling happiness so much that his first theme park, Disneyland, developed the reputation for being "the happiest place on Earth."

Mark Zuckerberg, the young billionaire who created Facebook, stated this about the mission he had: "Facebook was not originally created to be a company. It was built to accomplish a social mission, to make the world more open and connected."

The power behind this is that if you give your market a reason to get emotional about your business, to want to be a part of your success, to identify themselves as an extension of your team's overall goal, they will help to spread the message about your solution to many more people than if you are just selling products and services to make money.

An example of this can be seen with many organic grocery stores. These types of stores have a mission regarding personal health and the sustainability of our planet—paper bags vs. plastic bags, etc.—as a result, their customers are also passionate about these same goals and spread news of their support excitedly.

A mission should tap into the emotions and passions of the target market. It should represent and say just as much about its customers as it does the company. Someone who purchases your products and services will then also show a sign of support for what your company is trying to achieve: the common good that you have in mind, a focus on either improving the industry or—at a larger scale—the country, the world, etc.

Let's break it down into a simple action plan now.

YOUR 3-STEP ACTION PLAN FOR CHAPTER THREE:

1. Answer the questions. The success and profitability of your business idea relies on your being able to not only explain why someone should spend money on your idea instead of the other options available to them, but it must also have a moat built around it to prevent copycats from stealing it. If you can't answer why someone should spend money on your business idea, and if you have nothing to stop anyone from just copying it and doing it themselves, then you'll be in rocky territory very quickly.

These two questions are the first questions I ask any entrepreneur who approaches me for consulting help to market their "great new business idea."

2. Prove your claim. The market will be skeptical of any big, exciting, and new promises you make to them regarding your new products and services. It's not enough to say that your solution offers a superior advantage over competitors – you must prove it.

3. Have a bigger purpose. Give your market a reason to want to cheer for your continued success. Simply wanting to make money off of them will not help you in the long run. Strive to build your idea—your business as a whole—around a bigger goal.

Do you want to disrupt the current industry norms because you believe the market deserves better? Do you have a charitable cause you want your business to support? Do you want to create world peace? Save the environment? You get the idea. Let your market know what you're striving to achieve so they can rally behind your cause too.

Now that you have a great understanding of the secret to profitable business ideas, you may be thinking of closing this book and just getting started. Don't do that. Why? Because just having a unique advantage alone won't get the market to buy from you.

To help get sales rolling in faster for your new product or service, you'll need...

Chapter Four:

The Missing Link to Success

THIS CHAPTER, WHILE not immediately as exciting a concept as the previous two, is very important in your overall success with any business ideas you are looking to implement. It will allow you to do what is probably the hardest thing in any business transaction: get the prospect to take action and buy.

With the information in this chapter, you'll learn about the biggest obstacle in persuading a prospect in your market to spend money on your new business idea. You'll also learn how to gain more control of your market using a very simple approach to how you do business.

SOME ITEMS I COVER IN THIS CHAPTER:

a) The reason many profitable ideas with potential end up failing when they go to market

b) A great lesson which can be learned by studying late night informercials

c) What business and sex have in common and why you need to be cautious

d) The primary thought that will be on your prospect's mind whenever you offer to help them

e) Why you should view your breakthrough idea as if it were on a scale

Now let's dive in to the content.

The reason many potentially profitable ideas end up failing—even when they properly utilize the secret I shared with you—is due to the fact that a profitable idea on its own won't necessarily sell itself. This is mainly a result of the inherent skepticism and other potential objections to making a buying decision that your prospects will naturally have.

Have you ever looked at an ad or watched a commercial and thought that the product just seemed too good to be true? That is how a large portion of your market will respond to your initial promise of an amazing new solution with a never-before-seen advantage. They will be skeptical. They will want to know what the "catch" is.

THE BIGGEST CHALLENGE YOU WILL ENCOUNTER

You must conquer the initial fears and concerns that cause your prospects to hesitate in buying your products and services.

I compare it to a scale, like a scale of justice. If you're giving your prospective customer infinitely more reasons to say yes than no—infinitely more reasons to go forward than be tentative or contemplative—then you will see more of them taking you up on your offer.

Anytime any two individuals come together in any form for any kind of a transaction—business, employment, romance, sex, etc.—one side is always asking the other, either verbally or non-verbally, consciously or subconsciously, implicitly or explicitly, to take on all, most, or more of the risk in the transaction. And the risk is usually two kinds: There's the real risk and then there's the perceived risk.

What do you need to do to address this issue? You need to provide your market with an irresistible offer and remove any perceived risk associated with them taking action. You will need to eliminate as many hurdles as possible for the prospect in order to make your offer irresistible. Make it more appealing than unappealing.

Essentially you need to reverse risk for your prospective customers in everything you do so the downside is almost zero, and the upside nearly infinite. They should be able to believe in what you are telling them and trust you can help them, without fear of being ripped off in the end.

For example, if you had a business idea for a breakthrough new weight loss pill, you might say something along the lines of, "*I am so confident you will lose ten pounds and four inches off your stomach within the first three weeks, that I will give you double your money back if you aren't happy.*" Informercials commonly do this. Pay attention and you'll notice it constantly.

Everything needs to be geared towards making it easier, more attractive, and more appealing to say yes than no to your new product or service. Don't give your prospect any reason to need to think about it or to put off making a purchase decision. Make the offer so irresistible that it's next to impossible to say no to wanting it right now.

If you truly believe in the quality of your product or service, and believe that it will deliver exactly the advantages you say it will, then you should not be worried about any abuse of your offer to reduce risk on the prospect's side. The fact of the matter is that your prospect is more concerned about being scammed out of their money by you, than you should be of them taking advantage of you.

When it comes to making your offer as irresistible as possible, it boils down to providing as much value as you possibly can – an unbelievable amount of value that the prospect would move mountains just to take you up on it.

It costs a fortune to attract a new client or customer in the first place, but it costs very little to resell them again in the future. So you want to get them to become a customer as quickly as possible to make money for future repeat sales—which we'll expand on more in Chapter 7: Bulletproof Your Business.

YOUR 3-STEP ACTION PLAN FOR CHAPTER FOUR:

1. Identify hurdles. Before you can expect your market to stampede in your direction to purchase your products or services, you must first address any concerns and objections they would have in doing so. Failure to acknowledge these issues will result in your prospects delaying taking action, possibly permanently.

2. Remove the risk. After identifying their primary objections, remove them. Explain to the market how you have removed any risk they have of being disappointed or feeling ripped off by taking you up on your offer. Let them know you truly stand behind the advantage you promise them with your product or service.

3. Make it irresistible. Package the pitch for your product or service in such a way that the prospect can't help but become excited about the opportunity to buy it. If you don't convey your business idea in such a way that it excites the prospect, they won't have any desire to take action. A truly irresistible offer can make someone with even a slight interest in what your idea can deliver to want it that much more.

Once you have determined what offer can be made to persuade the largest number of prospects to become customers or clients, it is time to move to the most important element in minimizing your risk moving forward. It's time for…

Chapter Five:
Collect and Capture

YOU'VE DONE YOUR research, crafted your solution, and made it irresistible. Now comes the real test: collecting feedback. Far too many excited business owners are so in love with their own ideas that they rush to do a massive rollout of the idea, but they do it without first ensuring the market will respond to it favourably.

This chapter focuses on what issues and approaches you need to be aware of before doing a massive push of your idea, and how to minimize your financial and emotional risk in the process. This will allow you to confidently try out more ideas in a controlled manner, and prevent you from feeling it's an all-or-nothing situation each time.

SOME ITEMS I COVER IN THIS CHAPTER:

a) The two words that may save you many millions of dollars later

b) How trips to a local shoe store turned into an $8 billion empire

c) How to fail in a way that's extremely profitable

d) The three questions you must ask anyone who encounters your idea

e) What you can do yourself that Facebook has spent billions on

Now let's dive into the content.

Assuming how the market will respond to your new business idea can be a costly mistake if you end up missing the mark. It makes much more sense to do a market test. Go straight to the target market and find out exactly what they think about your offer, including the advantage it includes and the risk removal you provide.

In Chapter 2: Find the Flaws, I stated that relying on your friends and family for their feedback can be a recipe for disaster because they don't have to verify their opinion by actually spending money. This is the time to actually see how the market will truly respond, whether they are willing to spend money on what you have to offer.

This is an approach used by successful—and clearly financially prudent—companies. In fact, you may have heard about a little American online retail store by the name of Zappos. Founded in 1999 by Nick Swinmurn, this company had the "wild idea" of trying to sell shoes online.

Nick had done his research and found that footwear in the United States was a 40 billion-dollar market, and 5% of that market was being sold via paper mail order catalogs. Nick approached the venture capital team of Tony Hsieh (pronounced 'Shay') and Alfred Lin with his idea, and they were very interested in the concept; however, they had doubts whether people would dare to order shoes over the Internet back in the late 90s.

THE BILLION DOLLAR TEST

In Hsieh's book, "Delivering Happiness," he describes the quick market test they decided to run. They set up a basic website with shoe images taken from manufacturer's websites, added some order buttons, and waited to see what happened.

Cha-ching! An order would come through, and one of the team members would run to the local shoe store and buy the requested items at full retail. He would then rush back home and ship the order. Did they lose money on every order doing this test? You bet. Had the test failed, they would have lost a lot more money had they just dove right on in to their idea.

However, as a result of this small early test, they were able to ascertain that the idea was very much a viable business idea. Within eight years, the company grew to generate over $1 billion a year in annual revenue and an eventual acquisition by Amazon for $1.2 billion.

As I've mentioned previously in this book, think and move quickly. It's all about speed of implementation in your ideas. It's better to fail fast, if you're going to fail at all, as it saves you a lot of wasted time and resources.

Determining whether your market will actually respond to what you have to offer is your main priority before you do anything else moving forward after idea conception. This isn't just limited to the business owner though. Even as an investor, like with previous story involving Tony Hsieh and Alfred Lin, you can approach the market by first testing whether an idea you're thinking of investing in would fly.

The whole point of this is to minimize or even eliminate risk if the market displays no buying behaviour or interest. Put up even something as simple as a dummy website, similar to the Zappos example, to see if the market would actually try and buy what you have to offer if you offered it.

See if the solution—with the advantages you created—is the solution the market had in mind and wants. If there is a lack of interest at this stage, go back to the drawing board. Repackage your solution, improve upon the advantages, do additional market research – do whatever is needed to start seeing a positive response from the market. Do not waste time and money.

Another way you can collect feedback directly from the market is to request or offer to create trial access or beta testers of your new product or service. This has two benefits: You are able to see how much interest there is in your idea, and you also get to obtain reviews and social proof once the initial users show how happy they are with your idea.

Also, this collection of feedback should not just be a one-time occurrence. You should always strive to collect feedback from customers and clients as you continue forward. Have an idea of what the market truly thinks about what you have to offer, and react accordingly to the information you receive.

There are three primary questions you will want to ask your trial testers of your new business idea, concept, product, or service:

1) What do you like about (product / service / the business)?
2) What don't you like about (product / service / the business)?
3) What's the ONE THING that would improve (product / service / the business)?

By asking these three questions, you will not only have an idea of what is working with your business idea, but you will also be given much more information to identify where there is room for improvement. This room for improvement is what a competing company would want to utilize to take those customers away from you. Instead, use it to your advantage to further strengthen the figurative moat you have built around your business idea.

These questions can also be utilized in your future market research of competing businesses in any industry. It will help you to easily find the flaws that will give you an appealing advantage over your competition.

Another benefit in collecting feedback and tracking interest from the market is that it gives you an incredible opportunity to build a list of contacts to whom you can make offers later, individuals who have clearly shown an interest in the type of solutions you have to offer, but now with direct contact access to them. This will allow you to potentially skip expensive middlemen like traditional media to make future offers to them.

Facebook has been known to buy companies just based on their user base to have access to that list of contacts. Imagine if Zappos had set up a website announcing a new shoe concept being designed, and had interested visitors enter their contact information for future announcements. That list of names would then become very valuable to any shoe manufacturer that Zappos then approaches to have a shoe created for them. They will have verified the market demand exists for the product in advance, and without the capital investment required ahead of time.

YOUR 3-STEP ACTION PLAN FOR CHAPTER FIVE:

1. Check for interest. Establish some sort of prototype or demo environment that you can promote to your target market and then gauge interest in the solution you have planned. This can be in the form of taking pre-orders for the solution you are working for, either at a significantly discounted rate for their willingness to take action before the product is ready or simply adding their name to a list of people who would be interested in buying or trying it. It's best to do this before you invest a ton of time and money into the actual production of your idea.

2. Ask for feedback. Once you have customers or clients utilizing your new product or service, or at least have had the opportunity to review what it will be all about, it is time to collect their feedback on it. You want to fail fast if your idea is going to fail at all, and then make the necessary improvements to make it ready to go. Use the three primary questions that I shared with you previously.

3. Build a list. As you are attracting interested individuals to the promises your solution offers, and especially when you begin collecting feedback from them, it's crucial that you keep a list of those contacts so you can directly follow up with them in the future. Those who provide feedback for this idea may be willing to do so with future ideas as well. They may also be the first in line to buy similar solutions in line with the results your idea is promising to deliver.

Now that you have been given the proverbial green light in terms of moving forward with your business idea at full speed, it's time that you were shown…

Chapter Six:
The Five Crucial Systems to Implement

IN THE FIRST chapter of this book, I mentioned that you want to avoid the trap of creating a job for yourself, a prison of your own making, created in your attempt to pursue the freedom of becoming a business owner, and the joy that being your own boss is supposed to bring.

You'll benefit from this chapter as it will help keep you as far away from that pitfall as possible. It will allow you to pursue your passion for this profitable idea, knowing that you won't be held captive by it. The information in this chapter will help to prevent you from draining all your time and energy on something other than the areas of your life that mean the most to you.

SOME ITEMS I COVER IN THIS CHAPTER:

a) The three elements of a business built with solid systems

b) How to unlock a never-ending flow of new referrals and sales for your business

c) The #1 concern your prospects will have when they talk about your business

d) A system that many businesses owners drop the ball on, which leaves them vulnerable

e) What your clients and customers can give you to help you dominate your industry

Let's get started.

Have you—or someone you know—been so excited by a business idea that you spent hundreds of hours making it a reality? Once it became a reality, you realized it then required sweat, blood and tears to continue to be operational, eventually draining you, its creator, of all your time and energy. This is the sad reality for many aspiring entrepreneurs.

Now if this is your thing, all the power to you, but if it's not, let me help ensure you can avoid such a fate. The reason many business owners end up getting themselves into trouble is due to their failure to utilize systems within the business.

Sure, they may have delivery systems and accounting systems, but those are just a few operational systems. What about systems to ensure the business can continue to bring in new sales, continue to grow, and continue to thrive, without the business owner needing to be present to do all the work?

Let's discuss the crucial systems you must implement to ensure your business idea has a successful foundation moving forward. Systems are your greatest leverage within a business. Make sure you implement consistent systems and processes into your business idea to ease future scalability of the concept, and so that the business can run without you.

Actually, my company—Unique Profit Systems Inc.—was started due to my belief in the importance of leveraging systems. By utilizing proven marketing and selling systems for my small business consulting clients, I am able to help them increase their sales by 30% or more in as little as 30 days, guaranteed.

THE MAGIC TO ATTRACTING
BUYERS AND INVESTORS

Solid systems provide consistency, reliability, and sustainability. This is what makes proven franchises so desirable to certain entrepreneurs. It allows them to take a business idea that is already working in one location to a new market area, and have it work just as well without requiring them to be the ones doing all the work.

In order for you to truly be able to step away from your business idea and have it continue to run profitably, you require the following five systems:

First off, you need to create a system for attracting and collecting new leads. A business without leads constantly in the pipeline will struggle. Find a way to systematize this process so that your business is able to consistently generate additional leads on autopilot.

The second system you need to implement is one for stimulating referrals and repeat purchases from within your customer or client base. By having a system in place to do this, you will find that every new individual that spends money on your business idea is worth much more in terms of the additional new sales they bring in as well.

Your ability to generate the second system will be greatly based on your ability to deliver a consistent customer experience to your market. They need to know that anyone they refer to you, or any future purchases they make, will be almost exactly the same as the initial experience they had. In order to do this, you will need to ensure you implement a system for delivering that consistency.

The third system is exactly that: a system to ensure a remarkable customer experience. Your ability to generate a great deal of word-of-mouth advertising regarding your business idea will be largely based on the first impression you create with your new clients.

What first impression do you want clients and customers to have when they experience what you have to offer? How will you ensure this impression happens every single time with every new customer and with every purchase they make?

A system that especially confirms great customer service can turn customers into an army of raving fans who tell everyone they encounter about you. They must feel confident in what they refer to people they care about.

The fourth system you need to implement is a process for asking for testimonials and reviews from the satisfied clients that do business with you. You can leverage these in a multitude of ways to further strengthen your lead generation and enhance your referral generation as well.

The fifth and final system you need to design and implement into your business idea is one for training your staff. You need to have a documented process and method for educating new staff on the advantage and mission of your business, and how the consistent delivery of the product or service works.

Let's break it down.

YOUR 3-STEP ACTION PLAN FOR CHAPTER SIX:

1. Get consistent results. Before you can implement systems into your business, you need to make sure that they will actually create the results you want them to. The initial startup of your business idea will require a lot of trial and error until you get the right end result within each area every single time.

2. Document the process. Once you have achieved the consistency in results that you have been looking for, it is time to document the process. You should document every single step in a way that if you have to step away from the business, or if someone else wanted to franchise your idea, it could be done properly each and every time.

Having your systems set up properly also ensures that your business is never dependent on a single individual. If someone were to suddenly up and quit, or become sick, your business should be able to continue to deliver the same expected results to the market. Investors get nervous when the success of a business idea is riding solely on key persons.

3. Implement and improve. Once you have documented the process, it is time to make sure that someone else can take your instructions and execute them as you had planned. If the instructions aren't clear, or the results they are producing for the respective system isn't as desired, then you must continue to tweak and improve upon the various system designs until they are running like clockwork.

With the peace of mind and freedom that you will finally have with these systems, you can now proceed to the next section. Here's where we make your business idea a force that stands the test of time. This is where you discover the power of…

Chapter Seven:

Bulletproofing Your Business

THE INFORMATION IN this chapter will prevent you from experiencing a variety of different profit leaks which can erode your business' sales and morale. By addressing these issues, and plugging these leaks, you will be able to gain more control over the success of your business in the long term.

By the time you are finished reading this chapter, I have no doubt that you will understand why your business will truly feel bulletproofed.

SOME ITEMS I COVER IN THIS CHAPTER:

a) How to help a struggling company utilize business first aid

b) Why promoting the fact you have great customer service is hurting you

c) The one thing every business must have to establish long-term profitability

d) How to sell more products and services to customers and have them love you for it

e) The magic behind selling solutions below cost and still generating large profit increases

Now let's dive into the content.

When I refer to bulletproofing, I do not mean the ability to literally stop bullets, though that would be a very interesting strategy to add in. I'm referring to the various tactics and concepts you'll need to have working in your favour to make your business truly unstoppable.

Just like how an injury that is perceived to be minor can cause continuous blood loss until a person dies, so too can allowing seemingly small profit leaks to eat away at your business until it can no longer survive.

In this chapter, I'll address three of the most common "business bullets" I've come across, and what you can do to solidify your business to stand against them, thus protecting your business from both economic and industry fluctuations. Pay close attention to this information. You can use it to not only save your own business, but to also seal the fate of competitors who aren't structured to defend against them.

BULLET #1 – CUSTOMER/CLIENT ATTRITION

The first bullet to avoid is the business killer known as attrition – more specifically, customer or client attrition, or the number of clients that have stopped doing business with you. The most overlooked opportunity in every business to maximize profits is in preventing attrition of your existing customer base. Seriously.

How much time and money would be spent to replace the customers who leave just to maintain your existing sales? To increase your sales, you would have to not only replace the clients that stopped frequenting your business; you would also need to attract additional ones.

As you can now see, by reducing the number of customers and clients that stop doing business with you, and thereby minimizing the number of individuals you need to attract just to maintain existing sales, it's almost as if you did generate additional new customers into your business.

With that said, here are the three main reasons why most of us will cease doing business with someone:

Reason #1 - We no longer require or gain a benefit from products or services they are providing. Whether it is retail, residential, commercial, you name it. If your customer no longer feels like what you have to offer is helping them to achieve what they need, they will not spend any more money with you.

Reason #2 – We had an unsatisfactory experience with the product, service, or business staff in general. I'm sure you can relate to this. Have you ever had a negative experience at a restaurant? Store? A service provider? You may not have said it out right, but most likely you have made a mental note never to spend money with that business again.

Reason #3 - A change occurred in our business or life that interrupted our buying practice with the business, and despite our willingness, we just never continued buying from them. We probably mean to, but just never get around to it. If we don't feel the company truly appreciates our business, it will only make us less concerned with feeling the need to frequent the business again sooner as well.

Now that we know the three main reasons for customer attrition, let's discuss how we can prevent it as much as possible in order to reduce the amount of work required to constantly replace lost business.

THERE ARE 3 PROVEN BUSINESS BOOSTERS

Remedy #1 - Start by following up with customers very shortly after they buy from you. This is also the time period when they will typically experience buyer's remorse, and considering requesting their money back for an impulse decision they are debating now. Following up with customers will allow you to address any concerns or dissatisfaction in their experience with your products, services, or staff.

This is also a great opportunity to refer back to the three primary questions from the initial feedback survey in Chapter 5: Collect and Capture. Do regular surveys of your clients, and reward those that participate in providing feedback to show your appreciation for their time.

Remedy #2 - The second area to dedicate resources towards is on quality customer service. Great customer service is very crucial for maintaining customers, lowering attrition, and stimulating repeat business.

Stating you have amazing customer service in your marketing does not make you special. It does not give you a unique advantage in the eyes of your market. Almost every business claims to have great customer service, and many of them truly do not. Quality service is not meant to be a selling point in attracting new customers.

Prove your commitment to quality service before, during, and after people buy from you. Let them tell people around them about the level of service you deliver via word of mouth. Your actions will speak louder—and be more credible—than anything you write about yourself. Simply focus your energy on the delivery of higher-than-expected levels of service.

Once again I'll refer to the book, "Delivering Happiness," by Zappos CEO Tony Hsieh. In the book, Hsieh explains that Zappos' formula for success was simply putting the customer first and offering delightful customer service. This is something that many businesses claim they do, but the difference between Zappos and most companies is the great lengths that Zappos will go to ensure a customer is always happy. Zappos manages to do so at a completely different level than almost everyone else, and has generated billions in sales as a result.

Remedy #3 - Keep in touch with your clients. This isn't complicated or time-consuming. Make offers to customers who haven't bought from you for some time to stimulate their desire to buy from you once again.

Communicate frequently with your customer base to nurture your relationships with them. You will strengthen their feeling of being acknowledged and appreciated by your business this way. Continue to build and reinforce the relationship and keep an open dialogue with your market. Most importantly, make sure you're listening for whatever problems or requests they have for solutions in their lives.

Andy Kurtzig is CEO of the website Pearl.com, which connects customers to lawyers, doctors, mechanics, and veterinarians who answer questions and dole out advice online. Andy devotes every Thursdays, all day, to cold-calling a portion of his current customers to learn more about who they are, and how and why they use his service. He doesn't reveal that he is the CEO to avoid having people feel the need to alter how they view the service, and so he is able to keep his fingers on the pulse of his market.

BULLET #2 – FOCUSING ON THE INITIAL SALE

The second bullet you need to defend against is leaving a ton of money on the table as a result of only focusing on acquiring the first sale. The majority of successful businesses realize they make real money only on repeat sales.

Along the same lines of Attrition Remedy #2 that I shared previously, you'll need to make the customer delighted enough to desire to purchase your product or service again. In any business, repeat business is where the real money lies. Remember this. It's also why it's usually much smarter to sell an ongoing product or service than a one-time solution.

How do you bulletproof your business from this profit killer? Simple. You need to build your backend. Have a process for stimulating repeat purchases by your customers and clients. One way you may choose to do this is by expanding your product and services to allow for multiple streams of income, making your business truly resistant to changes in the economy or your industry.

Another option, which you may commonly see during your own shopping experiences, is utilizing loss leaders by selling a product or service at cost or just below break-even. Remember my advice in Chapter 1: The Five Fatal Business Traps regarding the fatal flaw of attempting to compete simply based on having the lowest price? This is one way to avoid that trap. Have a plan to still make money, but have it be in the backend after you generate the initial sale.

Most businesses just rely on one primary source of revenue generation. This leaves them at a dangerous disadvantage should something affect that source. You must diversify. Build your business on multiple profit sources instead of depending on one single revenue-generating source. This also allows you to constantly optimize each of these sources for even greater returns.

The bottom line is that you must make growth thinking a natural part of your everyday business philosophy. Set specific and realistic target for your business, not just vague and generalized dreams.

BULLET #3 – FAILURE TO OFFER BENEFIT OPTIONS

The third bullet is failing to offer additional beneficial solutions to customers at the time of their purchase.

Implement upsells into your business strategy. Identify how you can offer the opportunity for an improvement, greater quantity, or upgrade to what your customers and clients are buying. What else can you suggest to give them better results, greater value or a better experience for what they are looking to achieve? Whatever upsells you create, make sure they continue to expand on the mission of the business. Continue to champion against the same problem.

This is where your systems from Chapter 6: Crucial Systems to Implement really come into play. Can you see how all these areas are interconnecting now? For example a quality referral system can still keep someone in the Reason #1 category engaged with your business even though they personally don't need the products and services.

Let's get you started implementing this now…

YOUR 3-STEP ACTION PLAN FOR CHAPTER SEVEN:

1. Reduce attrition. Attrition is definitely the cancer of the business world. It can be slow or fast, but if not dealt with properly, it will spread and cripple your business until it collapses. Doing whatever you can to minimize attrition will not only benefit you in terms of stopping loss, but will most likely stimulate new leads being generated due to the positive reputation you'll have within your market.

2. Stimulate repeat sales. Do not make the mistake of focusing solely on generating that initial sale, and then moving on to close the next. Work on strengthening the relationship with each client so that they continue to desire your products and services enough to make repeat purchases in the future.

3. Offer additional solutions. A prospect customer may approach you thinking they want Solution X, when you know that Solution X combined with Solution Y and Solution Z will give them even great results. You owe it to them to at least offer these additional products and services if it will help them achieve their desired goals in a more satisfactory manner. This satisfaction may lead them to want to purchase again from you in the future, and build loyalty to your business—connecting all three steps together.

Now that you have created a solid defence into your business strategy, let's look at how we can enhance your offence with…

Chapter Eight:

Tactics for Maximum Profits

IF YOU EVER plan to grow or expand your business, then you will want to pay close attention to this chapter. The information in this section will allow you to maximize your profits, while actually reducing your current expenses and practically eliminating your financial risk when adding new products and services to your business offerings.

By ignoring this information, you are setting your business up for a very costly game of "hope it works out" – Something that may lead to a lot of financial, emotional, and physical stress in your life.

SOME ITEMS I COVER IN THIS CHAPTER:

a) Why most business owners are taking a gamble every day

b) How to generate a 20-50% or more increase in your sales quickly and cheaply

c) Why your best marketing strategy really isn't as good as you think it is

d) One of the biggest mistakes businesses make when attempting to make changes

e) The best way to eliminate risk when rolling out new promotions or ideas

Now let's dive into the content.

Have you ever been told that starting your own business is risky? Have you ever been around a business owner who was distressed over losing a great sum of money due to a promotion or idea that failed to generate the results they expected? Yes? Good. Then you'll appreciate this chapter even more.

Most business owners treat their business efforts like marketing, and solution creation a lot like gambling, just hoping it pays off in the end. Unfortunately, they don't approach these efforts with the care and attention they need to. Your marketing, along with any new product and service creation, must be treated as a science. It must involve testing, analysis, and measuring of results that are generated.

What kind of elements should you be testing in regards to your business? Everything! Test a lot of suppositions that are foundationally based on marketing, moneymaking, business building, relationship-building science, and it doesn't matter if you lose on a few little things. When you find the winner, it's going to be so powerful.

YOU ONLY NEED TO CHANGE
A LITTLE TO PROFIT A LOT

Change the headline of your marketing materials, change the way you promise your advantage, change your price, change your bonus, change your risk reversal, change your benefits, etc. Any one of those changes singularly can increase the results you generate by 20, 30, 50% or more. A combination of multiple changes can just go off the chart in terms of results. But none of it will happen if you don't do tests on everything. This is a huge leverage opportunity.

When it comes to testing, you must only change one element at a time. If you test multiple changes at one time, you won't be able to identify what specific element resulted in the increase or decrease in sales that are generated. Use a strategy referred to as A/B testing or split testing. This is a tactic where you take one version of something, make a minor change to it, and then compare the results. Select the one which generated the best results as the winner, and now it's the control to be used against a new modified version.

It's always interesting when a business owner tells me they "tried" something and it didn't work, so now they have written it off as not being worth their effort. Trying something once does not immediately disqualify it if it generated even minor results. This is when I'll usually say, "Well, OK, tell me how many different ways you've tried it. Tell me how many different approaches you utilized."

Of course, with testing comes tracking of results. It is important that you not only track the results of every test you make, but every area of your business. Track trends in client demographics such as location, age, gender, number of employees, annual revenue, etc., as well as items purchased by your customers, the days they were purchased on, who they were with when they purchased, etc.

Information is a massive source of leverage as you move forward with your business. A database of contacts, including their interests, etc. is big money to anyone that understands the importance of targeting their market. Facebook and Google are infamous for their business models of data mining as much information as possible regarding their users to appeal to their advertisers better.

YOUR 3-STEP ACTION PLAN FOR CHAPTER EIGHT:

1. Split test. Test everything. Never stop testing. It's one of the fastest, most cost-efficient ways to create large jumps in your sales numbers. Identify what's working, and constantly try and find a way to improve upon it. Make it better. Make it more profitable. Rinse and repeat.

2. Test small. Whether it's a new product or service idea, or a new marketing or promotional effort, test small. Roll it out to a small sampling of your target market, or just a small quantity of product, and watch the results. If it's a failure, then at least you didn't put all of your eggs in one basket and lose your shirt in the end. If it produces profitable results, then you can begin to scale it up accordingly.

3. Track everything. With every test you do, track the results. Collect data on as much of your leads, customers, business partners, industry data, you name it. Track everything. Analyze the data and use it to improve the results of your future launches and activities as you move forward.

Now that you understand the necessity and power behind testing and tracking, let me show you how you can greatly increase your exposure to your market by taking advantage of...

Chapter Nine:
Profitable Partnerships

TRYING TO ACHIEVE success on your own is possible, but is definitely a lot harder. In this chapter I'll share not only why you should want to learn how to implement profitable partnerships, but also the best way to accomplish this task.

Knowing the strategies and techniques in this chapter will not only allow you to rapidly increase the amount of exposure you're able to achieve for your products and services, but it will also help to prevent you from tapping into your limited resources when you can avoid it.

SOME ITEMS I COVER IN THIS CHAPTER:

a) How to get other companies to promote you for FREE

b) The one question you must ask when looking to create a joint venture

c) What you must provide every business you approach to partner with you

d) The information you need to know before you even consider a joint venture

e) What you can give away for free to greatly increase your sales

Now let's dive into the content.

One of the biggest walls many aspiring entrepreneurs and new business owners face is lack of capital to help generate exposure for their new products or services. But what if you didn't need to spend a ton of money to get that exposure? Would that be of interest to you?

The answer to nearly unlimited exposure for very little cost lies in two simple words: profitable partnerships. Perhaps you are familiar with the term joint venture? This is when two businesses come together for a mutually beneficial arrangement.

Often regarded as highly sought after and hard to accomplish, profitable partnerships are a very lucrative source of leverage if done properly. Unfortunately, many business owners get this wrong, and as a result do find joint ventures to be very hard to establish and implement.

HERE IS THEY KEY TO
CREATING JOINT VENTURES

At the heart of any partnership is an understanding of give and take, the ability to give back as much or more value to the other person as you receive from them. Just like with many romantic relationships, joint ventures often fail due to business representatives only thinking about their own needs. The biggest mistake you can make when trying to establish joint venture opportunities is telling them what you want rather than asking what they want. You want to give help before you try to get help.

I came across a great example of this in my research of successful marketing strategies. Long ago, Walt Disney wanted something special done for the new Abraham Lincoln part of Disneyland. There was one animatronics expert he had in mind that could give him what he wanted, so he sent his executives out to recruit this man for the project. They came back empty-handed, telling Walt that the expert had said he was too busy at the time and couldn't be bought.

Walt was undeterred. He said to his executives, *"Did you ask him what he needs or wants, but can't get?"* They said, *"No."* Walt then said, *"Go back and ask him that."* As it turns out, he needed $50 million for a research facility. Upon discovering this information, Walt said to his executives, *"Well, give him that. We can do that."* The end result: Both the expert and Walt got what they wanted.

What can you take away from this example? Simply that the right question which opens the door for a joint venture opportunity is "What can we do for you? What do you want? What do you need that you can't get?" This can lead you to custom-creating something, a product or service for that potential partner which gets you in front of their audience – a mutually beneficial relationship.

When you are just starting out with your business idea, you will probably have very little in terms of finances to promote yourself with. It's then very important that you understand what the marginal net worth, the lifetime value of a buyer, is to your business. In other words, what is the stream of profit that predictably would result from getting that first sale, and the many additional purchases that could follow? Refer back to Chapter 7: Bulletproofing Your Business.

Once you have calculated out the average amount of total profit which will be generated from the average customer or client, you can now give away all the front money, all the first purchases, to somebody else for generating the sale for us. Essentially you offer a large portion—or all—of the initial sale profits to your partner in exchange for them allowing you to access their customer base. As long as you are still profitable in the backend sales, it does not matter that you give up the initial sales, especially when they are sales you would not have gotten without the partnership existing.

THIS IS WHERE PEOPLE GO WRONG

As I mentioned earlier, profitable partnerships are relationships at their core. Unfortunately, most people don't leverage their relationships properly. They exploit them negatively, focusing only on getting as much as possible for themselves with no concern for what the other party gains from it. This is probably, with no disrespect to network marketing, the greatest crash and burner of relationships I've ever seen.

If you look around you in your day-to-day activities, you will most likely see joint ventures everywhere: New vehicles coming with an initial free trial of satellite radio services; Starbucks coffee shops inside of book stores and retail outlets; children's toy companies having their toys packed together within fast food restaurant meal options for kids; airline companies partnering with credit card companies to offer discount flights to those who use their credit cards to accumulate points, etc.

Redbox Automated Retail LLC was founded in 2002, and started off by having 11 DVD rental kiosks placed within local area grocery stores. Fast forward a decade later, and in 2013 the company had grown to over 42,000 kiosks at more than 34,000 locations. This has given Redbox a whopping 47.8% of the physical rental market. This is just one of many companies whose entire business growth model is based around profitable partnerships with host locations.

It is all about finding companies who have customers whom could benefit by what your solution provides, and positioning your solution for them in a positive light to a potential partner that already caters to that same target audience.

Also, don't be fooled into thinking that just promising untold fortunes upon a business if they partner with you will magically make them jump with excitement to work with you. This will especially be least effective with successful people because they don't need your money.

THE SAME RULE FOR SUCCESS APPLIES HERE TOO

Find out what they want, and show them how you can help them get it. Does this sound familiar? Probably because it's the same proven advice for appealing to profitable markets which I shared with you in Chapter 2: Find the Flaws.

Another good thing to keep in mind is that potential partners want data. They want proof you will deliver a positive and profitable experience for both them and their client base. Don't approach potential partners until you have your own numbers for conversion and profits down pat. This will be the information that you began compiling in Chapter 8: Tactics for Maximum Profits. Once again, see how all of this is starting to flow together?

In your search for potential partners, you'll want to identify who has a sales force that's not competitive with you, but that reaches your market, and would love to have exclusive rights or access to something you can provide.

The ability to offer something exclusively—which their competitors cannot—will provide a potential partner with a unique advantage in their market. Remember Chapter 3: The Secret Unveiled? This is where you can squeeze yourself in if you communicate the benefit to them properly. Or maybe just buy them a copy of this book – whichever gets the job done.

You ability to provide value to a partner does not mean it has to cost you a lot either. You do not have to give away something that costs you to provide, like products and services. Instead, if you choose, you can simply give away content for them to provide to their audience, a guide or book that makes a valuable resource in the eyes of your partner's customer base, a resource which also recommends your products and services as a solution. This way everyone benefits from the value provided. Everyone wins.

This resource guide or informative media source can then be given away as a gift to your partner's customers after they make a purchase from your partner. It's like a bonus of sorts, which acts as ride-along value to the customer and does not take attention away from your partner's products or services until after the sales is done.

Make sense? Good. Here's what you'll need to do to get started…

YOUR 3-STEP ACTION PLAN FOR CHAPTER NINE:

1. Know your numbers. Before you even consider approaching a business to partner with them, you should know your own business data: how much the average client is worth over the lifetime of them doing business with you, what you cost-per-acquisition is typically for new leads, prospect to paying customer conversion rate, etc. This is information that will not only help you in your negotiations with partners, but will also be information that the partners will want to know as well most likely.

2. Identify partners. Know your target market and who the best companies you can approach are that also target those same individuals. These companies must not be in competition with you, or feel that you would take away from any potential sales they could make. The businesses your approach to partner with you must feel that you would make a natural fit with what they already offer their customer base.

3. Provide them value. Identify how you can help your partners to either sell more products or services, or enhance the results their customers will receive when they purchase products and services from your partner. Ideally you will create a solution that provides value and that is exclusive to your partner in order to make them that much more appealing in the eyes of your mutual market. The business must view being your partner as being extremely beneficial to them, or it will not happen.

You now have a solid foundation of strategies to build a very profitable business on. In the final chapter, I'll give you some things to keep in mind because it's time that you learned to…

Chapter Ten:

Dominate
Your Market

WITH THE STRATEGIES, concepts and action steps you've been provided over the last nine chapters, you have a serious arsenal of marketing weapons in your business war chest. Make them count. Put them to use as soon as possible.

If used properly, the ability to enter any industry, any market, and completely dominate the competition will be at your fingertips. Competitors who have fallen into the five fatal traps, or have failed to use the strategies you have been shown, won't stand much of a chance.

You have now begun discovering that many new opportunities for profitable ideas exist all around you. You consciously may have started identifying and finding the flaws in a variety of aspects you encounter throughout your day-to-day life. Welcome to the club.

SO WHAT HAPPENS NEXT?

Now you'll have the power to go out and start up a structured new business based off of your market research. Perhaps you'll work with existing businesses to improve their products and services. Heck, maybe you'll just sit back and locate quality businesses with proven business advantages to invest in. The possibilities are truly endless.

Hopefully by now you realize the great deal of power and knowledge you possess within this book. View yourself as more than just another business owner. Expand on it. Contribute and help to make others successful as you gain success. This way everyone wins.

MY MISSION:
MAKE A BILLION DOLLAR DIFFERENCE

I'm on a mission to help generate a billion dollars in new sales for businesses that implement the strategies I have now shared with you. The impact of this will be immense in the new jobs it creates, freedom it provides for families around the world, and perhaps even impacting the global economy if it spreads enough. Hopefully you can help to spread this information and help me make my desire to help more people a reality.

If you're like most people, you initially were intrigued by the concept of this book. You wanted to know the secret to profitable business ideas. By now, you realize that the secret to profitable business ideas is just the tip of a very large iceberg, one that, if built properly, can sink even the most Titanic-like of large corporations, catching them off guard by what lies behind the scenes of your rock-solid business idea.

While you began reading this book to discover just one secret to being successful, hopefully you now realize that it is, in fact, just one piece of a much larger profit puzzle, a puzzle that you can expand into being as simple or complicated as you desire. The answer I'm giving you to the secret lies within your ability to not only dream big but also to take immediate action on your ideas.

BUT I HAVE A CONFESSION TO MAKE

Yes, as hard as this may be to believe, this book is far from perfect. In fact, it's not even as comprehensive as I'd like it to be. I could have expanded on every chapter in this book—double, triple, or quadrupled the information you have just received with even more details and case studies—and it would still only barely scratch the surface of profitable possibilities.

You see, I've been studying marketing and business strategies since 2007, and I wanted to create a basic resource that I could provide to anyone and watch them obtain profitable results. Despite the incredible results that will be generated for most businesses using these strategies, it's still just a basic resource. There's a lot more that I want to share with you to make your results even more incredible.

I want to make sure you have everything you need to be successful. For that reason, because you invested your time in this book, I am going to invest my time in doing whatever I can to make you a force to be reckoned with within your desired business industry.

YOUR FREE BONUS DETAILS BELOW

If you found the information in this book useful, then you'll be blown away by what I've decided to give you. I've created a series of bonuses worth well over $997 in value that I want you to access —*ABSOLUTELY FREE*—as a reader of my book. *No strings attached, nothing to buy, they are yours to access at no additional cost.* All I ask is that you don't share it with others who have not committed the time and resources to completing this book as you have. Deal?

Head to the website below to access your bonuses:
http://www.secrettoprofitableideas.com/dexxbonus

These bonuses will contain advanced marketing and business strategies to take your sales and company growth to all new levels, optimizing them for maximum efficiency and effectiveness. Ensuring you get the greatest return on investment possible from all areas of your business.

Some of these strategies will be concepts and techniques that I also share with my private consulting clients, the businesses that I help to grow their sales by 30% or more in as little as 30 days, guaranteed. Now you'll be able to utilize some of these high-level concepts within your own business as you move forward.

However, don't delay on accessing these bonuses. If I find the bonus link has been compromised, I will have to disable access to the page without warning. Hopefully by the time you are reading this, it has not happened. Head over to the website now and claim your access immediately.

Once again, visit the website below to access your bonuses:
http://www.secrettoprofitableideas.com/dexxbonus

As I said before, the information you received in this book is a great start to building an incredibly profitable business. However, I want to take you to the next level. I'm excited to see your results with the advanced training, combined with what you achieve using the strategies in this book.

Thank you again for your time and support of this book. Be sure to let others know about it, especially those you feel will also benefit from discovering the secret to profitable business ideas.

Also, **please leave a review at Amazon.com about this book**, and let others know what an impact this information will have on the way you do business moving forward.

Cheers to your future success!

Sincerely,

Dexx Williams